Parenting with Purpose Nurturing Your Child's Potential

Jack Musa

Parenting with Purpose Nurturing Your Child's Potential
Copyright © 2023 by Jack Musa

The first edition was published in 2023

ISBN:
Published by:
Sunshine
1663 Liberty Drive
Hyderabad, IN 47403
www.Sunshinepublishers.com

This book is self-published using on-demand printing and publishing, which allows it to be printed and distributed globally.

TABLE OF CONTENTS

Chapter 1: Understanding Parenting with Purpose

Defining Parenting with Purpose

Parenting is a journey that comes with great responsibilities but also offers immense rewards. It is a role that requires dedication, love, and a clear purpose. In this subchapter, we delve into the concept of "Parenting with Purpose," exploring what it means and how it can enhance your relationship with your child.

Parenting with Purpose is about consciously and intentionally nurturing your child's potential. It goes beyond the day-to-day tasks of providing for their physical needs and delves into the realm of guiding their emotional, intellectual, and moral development. It involves being present, engaged, and proactive in shaping their future.

To parent with purpose, you must first understand and embrace your role as a parent. Recognize that you are more than just a caretaker; you are their mentor, guide, and biggest advocate. Your purpose is to provide a loving and supportive environment where your child can flourish and become the best version of themselves.

Defining your purpose as a parent requires reflection and self-awareness. What values do you want to instill in your child? What skills and qualities do you hope they will possess? By identifying these aspirations, you can create a roadmap that will guide your parenting decisions and actions.

Parenting with Purpose also means fostering a strong bond with your child. This involves spending quality time together, actively listening to them, and being genuinely interested in their thoughts and feelings. By building a solid foundation of trust and open communication, you can better understand their needs and provide the necessary guidance.

Furthermore, Parenting with Purpose entails setting clear boundaries and expectations. Children thrive when they have structure and consistency in their lives. By establishing rules and consequences, you help them develop a sense of responsibility, self-discipline, and respect for others.

Lastly, Parenting with Purpose involves recognizing and nurturing your child's unique talents and interests. Encourage them to explore their passions, offer support, and provide opportunities for growth and learning. By doing so, you empower them to discover their true potential and pursue their dreams.

In conclusion, Parenting with Purpose is a conscious and intentional approach to raising children. It requires defining your role as a parent, building a strong bond, setting boundaries, and nurturing your child's individuality. By embracing this mindset, you can create a nurturing and empowering environment that allows your child to reach their full potential.

The Importance of Nurturing Your Child's Potential

As parents, our primary goal is to raise happy, healthy, and successful children. We want to provide them with every opportunity to thrive and reach their full potential. Nurturing your child's potential is an essential aspect of parenting, as it sets the foundation for their future success.

Every child is born with unique talents, abilities, and potential. It is our responsibility as parents to recognize and cultivate these gifts, helping our children discover their passions and interests. By doing so, we empower them to pursue their dreams and develop the skills necessary to excel in their chosen endeavors.

Nurturing your child's potential involves creating an environment that fosters growth and learning. It means providing them with opportunities to explore various activities, whether it's through music, sports, art, or academics. By exposing them to different experiences, we allow them to discover their strengths and interests.

Encouragement and support are critical in nurturing your child's potential. As parents, we need to be their biggest cheerleaders, providing them with positive reinforcement and believing in their abilities. By doing so, we instill confidence in them, which is vital for them to take risks and overcome challenges.

Furthermore, it is essential to create a balanced approach to nurturing your child's potential. While it is crucial to encourage their interests and passions, it is equally important to expose them to a well-rounded education. This includes providing them with opportunities to develop social skills, emotional intelligence, and critical thinking abilities. By nurturing a holistic set of skills, we equip our children with the tools they need to succeed in all aspects of life.

Additionally, nurturing your child's potential involves fostering a growth mindset. It is essential to teach them that failure is not the end but an opportunity to learn and grow. By teaching them resilience and perseverance, we help them develop the mindset necessary to overcome obstacles and achieve their goals.

In conclusion, nurturing your child's potential is a fundamental aspect of parenting. By recognizing and cultivating their unique talents and abilities, providing them with opportunities to explore and learn, and offering unwavering support and encouragement, we empower our children to reach their full potential. Remember, every child is capable of greatness, and it is our role as parents to help them unlock their true potential and guide them toward a fulfilling and successful future.

The Role of Parents in Shaping Their Child's Future

Parenting is one of the most important and rewarding jobs in the world. As parents, we have the power to shape our children's future and help them reach their full potential. In this subchapter, we will explore the crucial role parents play in nurturing their child's potential.

First and foremost, parents are their child's first teachers. From the moment they are born, children look up to their parents for guidance and learn by observing their actions. It is our responsibility to set a positive example and instill important values in our children. By modeling empathy, respect, and perseverance, we can teach our children valuable life skills that will benefit them throughout their lives.

Additionally, parents have the power to create a nurturing and supportive environment for their children. The home is where a child's personality and character begin to take shape. By providing a loving and secure environment, we can help our children develop a strong sense of self-esteem and confidence. This, in turn, will help them face challenges and overcome obstacles later in life.

Furthermore, parents play a crucial role in their child's education. While schools have a significant impact on a child's academic development, parents are their child's first and most important educators. By encouraging a love for learning, actively participating in their education, and providing support and guidance, parents can help their child excel academically and set them on a path to success.

Moreover, parents have the responsibility to identify and nurture their child's talents and interests. Each child is unique, with their own set of strengths and passions. By paying attention to their interests and providing opportunities for them to explore and develop these talents, parents can help their child discover their true potential and pursue their dreams.

Lastly, parents have the power to instill important life skills in their children. From teaching them essential values such as honesty and responsibility to equipping them with essential skills like problem-solving and decision-making, parents play a crucial role in preparing their children for the challenges of adulthood.

In conclusion, parents have a significant role to play in shaping their child's future. By being positive role models, creating a nurturing environment, actively participating in their education, nurturing their talents, and instilling important life skills, parents can help their children grow into successful, confident, and well-rounded individuals. Parenting is a journey filled with love, dedication, and purpose, and by embracing our role as parents, we can make a profound impact on our child's future.

Chapter 2: Building a Strong Foundation

Establishing a Loving and Supportive Environment

One of the most important aspects of parenting is creating a loving and supportive environment for your child to thrive in. As parents, we have the power to shape our child's world and influence their emotional and psychological development. In this subchapter, we will explore the key elements of establishing such an environment, and how it can positively impact your child's potential.

First and foremost, it is crucial to create a strong emotional connection with your child. This connection forms the foundation of a loving and supportive environment. Spend quality time with your child, engage in meaningful conversations, and actively listen to their thoughts and feelings. Show empathy, validate their emotions, and provide them with a safe space to express themselves. By doing so, you are building trust and nurturing a strong parent-child bond.

Additionally, it is important to establish clear and consistent boundaries. Children thrive in an environment where they feel secure and know what is expected of them. Set age-appropriate rules and consequences, and ensure that they are communicated effectively. However, it is equally important to balance boundaries with flexibility and understanding. Allow your child to make mistakes and learn from them, while providing guidance and support along the way.

Creating a positive and nurturing environment also involves fostering open and honest communication. Encourage your child to express their thoughts, concerns, and dreams without fear of judgment. Be approachable, non-judgmental, and respectful of their opinions. By promoting open dialogue, you are teaching your child valuable communication skills and helping them develop a healthy sense of self-expression.

Furthermore, a loving and supportive environment involves modeling positive behavior. Children learn by observing their parents and imitating their actions. Be mindful of your own behavior, attitudes, and reactions. Demonstrate kindness, empathy, and respect in your interactions with others. Show your child how to handle conflicts, manage stress, and embrace diversity. By being a positive role model, you are teaching your child invaluable life skills that will shape their character.

In conclusion, creating a loving and supportive environment is essential for nurturing your child's potential. By establishing a strong emotional connection, setting clear boundaries, fostering open communication, and modeling positive behavior, you are providing your child with the foundation they need to flourish. Remember, as parents, we are the architects of our child's world, and by creating a nurturing environment, we are setting them up for a lifetime of success and happiness.

Setting Clear Boundaries and Expectations

In the journey of parenting, one of the most crucial aspects is setting clear boundaries and expectations for your child. As parents, it is our responsibility to guide and nurture our children's potential. By establishing firm boundaries and reasonable expectations, we provide them with a solid foundation for their growth and development. In this subchapter, we will explore the significance of clear boundaries and expectations and understand how to implement them effectively.

Setting boundaries is essential to help children understand their limits and develop self-discipline. It creates a safe and secure environment where they can explore, learn, and thrive. Boundaries enable children to differentiate between right and wrong, acceptable and unacceptable behavior. By setting consistent limits, parents can prevent their children from engaging in harmful activities and teach them the importance of respect and accountability.

To establish clear boundaries, it is crucial to communicate openly and honestly with your child. Explain the reasons behind the rules and restrictions, ensuring they understand the potential consequences of crossing those boundaries. This open dialogue fosters trust and mutual understanding, enabling children to internalize the importance of adhering to the boundaries set by their parents.

Alongside boundaries, expectations play a vital role in nurturing your child's potential. Expectations help children develop self-confidence and strive for excellence. However, it is crucial to set realistic and age-appropriate expectations to avoid overwhelming or discouraging your child. By setting achievable goals, parents can motivate their children to work hard, persevere, and grow.

Remember that every child is unique, and their abilities and interests may vary. Tailor your expectations accordingly, focusing on their strengths and supporting them in their areas of growth. Encourage open communication, where children can express their aspirations and concerns, allowing you to adjust expectations as needed.

Consistency is the key to effective boundary setting and expectation management. Ensure that both parents are on the same page and maintain a united front. Inconsistency can lead to confusion and frustration for children, making it difficult for them to understand and respect the boundaries and expectations set by their parents.

By setting clear boundaries and expectations, parents create an environment that fosters healthy growth and development. It promotes discipline, self-confidence, and a sense of responsibility in children. Remember, it is crucial to adapt boundaries and expectations as your child grows, ensuring they continue to nurture their potential and become well-rounded individuals.

Fostering Open Communication and Trust

One of the most crucial aspects of parenting is establishing open communication and trust with your child. As parents, it is our responsibility to create an environment where our children feel comfortable expressing their thoughts, feelings, and concerns. By fostering open communication and trust, we can build a strong foundation for a healthy parent-child relationship and nurture our child's potential.

To begin with, it is important to create a safe space for your child to share their thoughts and emotions. Encourage them to speak their mind without fear of judgment or punishment. Actively listen to what they have to say, giving them your undivided attention and showing genuine interest in their perspective. Avoid interrupting or dismissing their opinions, as this can discourage open communication.

Another essential factor in fostering open communication is practicing effective and empathetic communication yourself. Choose your words wisely and speak to your child in a respectful and understanding manner. Use active listening skills to ensure that you are truly comprehending their message. By modeling healthy communication, you are teaching your child how to express themselves effectively and respectfully.

Trust is a fundamental element in any relationship, and the parent-child bond is no exception. Building trust with your child requires consistency, honesty, and reliability. Keep your promises and be dependable, showing your child that they can rely on you. Be honest with them, even about difficult topics, as this will demonstrate that you value their trust and are willing to be open with them.

It is crucial to establish boundaries and rules within your household to ensure a sense of safety and security. However, it is equally important to involve your child in the decision-making process. Encourage them to share their thoughts and opinions when establishing rules, giving them a sense of ownership and responsibility. This collaborative approach helps in building trust and fostering open communication.

Finally, embrace and respect your child's individuality. Allow them to express their unique personality and interests without judgment. Celebrate their achievements, no matter how small, and provide constructive feedback when necessary. By accepting and supporting your child for who they are, you are creating an environment where they feel safe to be themselves and share their experiences openly.

In conclusion, fostering open communication and trust is vital for nurturing your child's potential. By creating a safe, non-judgmental space, practicing effective communication, building trust, involving your child in decision-making, and celebrating their individuality, you can establish a strong parent-child relationship. This foundation will not only help your child grow and thrive but will also enable you to guide them through life's challenges with love and understanding.

Chapter 3: Developing Positive Parenting Techniques

Encouraging Independence and Self-Confidence

As parents, one of our most important goals is to raise independent and confident children who can navigate the world with self-assurance and resilience. Encouraging independence and self-confidence in our children is a crucial aspect of parenting, as it equips them with the necessary skills and mindset to face challenges and strive for success. In this subchapter, we will explore various strategies and approaches that can help foster independence and self-confidence in your child.

First and foremost, it is essential to provide opportunities for your child to make decisions and take on responsibilities. Begin by giving them age-appropriate tasks such as making their bed or choosing their outfit for the day. As they grow older, gradually increase the complexity of the tasks, allowing them to take on more significant responsibilities. This not only builds their self-confidence but also teaches them valuable life skills.

Another crucial aspect is to allow your child to experience failure and learn from their mistakes. Instead of shielding them from every setback, encourage them to persevere and find solutions independently. This approach instills a growth mindset, teaching children that failures are stepping stones to success and that they have the ability to overcome challenges.

Furthermore, it is important to foster a supportive and nurturing environment where your child feels safe to explore their interests and express themselves. Offer encouragement and praise for their efforts, rather than solely focusing on the outcome. This helps build their self-esteem and reinforces their belief in their own abilities.

Additionally, teaching your child effective problem-solving and decision-making skills is crucial for their independence and self-confidence. Encourage them to think critically, explore different solutions, and evaluate the consequences of their choices. By equipping them with these skills, you are empowering them to make informed decisions and take ownership of their actions.

Lastly, model independence and self-confidence yourself. Your behavior serves as a powerful example for your child. Demonstrate resilience in the face of challenges, pursue your passions, and embrace opportunities for personal growth. By doing so, you are showing your child that independence and self-confidence are valuable traits to strive for.

In conclusion, encouraging independence and self-confidence in our children is a fundamental aspect of parenting. By providing opportunities for decision-making, allowing them to experience failure, fostering a supportive environment, teaching problem-solving skills, and modeling independence ourselves, we can help nurture their potential and prepare them for a successful and fulfilling future.

Implementing Effective Discipline Strategies

Discipline is an essential aspect of parenting that helps shape a child's behavior and instill important values. However, implementing effective discipline strategies can be a challenging task for parents. In this subchapter, we will explore practical and research-based approaches to discipline, providing you with valuable insights and techniques to nurture your child's potential.

One crucial aspect to consider when implementing discipline strategies is consistency. Consistency ensures that your child understands the consequences of their actions and helps establish clear boundaries. By consistently enforcing rules and expectations, you will create a sense of predictability and security for your child.

Another important aspect to keep in mind is the use of positive reinforcement. Instead of solely focusing on punishment, it is vital to acknowledge and reward your child's positive behavior. Praising and reinforcing desirable actions will encourage your child to continue exhibiting positive behavior, ultimately leading to better self-discipline.

When it comes to discipline, it is essential to set realistic expectations and age-appropriate consequences. Understanding your child's developmental stage will help you tailor your discipline strategies accordingly. For instance, younger children may require more guidance and redirection, while older children may benefit from logical consequences that directly relate to their actions.

Effective communication plays a significant role in discipline strategies. Instead of resorting to yelling or harsh punishments, strive to maintain open lines of communication with your child. By actively listening to their concerns and providing explanations for your disciplinary actions, you will foster a healthy parent-child relationship built on trust and mutual understanding.

Finally, it is crucial to lead by example. Children learn by observing their parents' behavior, so it is essential to model the values and behaviors you wish to instill in them. By demonstrating self-control, empathy, and respect, you will create a positive environment that promotes healthy discipline.

In conclusion, implementing effective discipline strategies is crucial for nurturing your child's potential. By maintaining consistency, using positive reinforcement, setting realistic expectations, practicing effective communication, and leading by example, you can create a nurturing and disciplined environment for your child to thrive. Remember, discipline should not be synonymous with punishment but rather an opportunity to teach valuable life lessons and shape your child's future.

Promoting Emotional Intelligence and Resilience

In the fast-paced and ever-changing world we live in today, it has become increasingly important for parents to focus on promoting emotional intelligence and resilience in their children. As parents, we want our children to grow up to be well-rounded individuals who can navigate life's challenges with confidence and grace. This subchapter aims to provide you with valuable insights and practical strategies on how to nurture emotional intelligence and resilience in your child.

Emotional intelligence refers to the ability to recognize, understand, and manage one's emotions effectively. By promoting emotional intelligence, we help our children develop better self-awareness, empathy, and interpersonal skills. One effective way to nurture emotional intelligence is by encouraging open communication and active listening at home. Create a safe and non-judgmental space where your child feels comfortable expressing their feelings and thoughts. Encourage them to talk about their emotions and validate their experiences. This will help them develop a better understanding of their own emotions and develop empathy towards others.

Resilience, on the other hand, is the ability to bounce back from setbacks and adversity. It is a crucial skill that will enable your child to face life's challenges head-on and learn from them. One way to foster resilience is by allowing your child to experience failure and disappointment. While it is natural for parents to want to protect their children from pain, shielding them from failure can hinder their ability to develop resilience. Instead, offer support and guidance when they face setbacks, helping them understand the importance of perseverance and learning from their mistakes.

Teaching problem-solving and coping skills is another effective strategy to promote emotional intelligence and resilience. Encourage your child to think critically and find solutions to their own problems. Teach them healthy coping mechanisms such as deep breathing exercises, journaling, or engaging in physical activities. By equipping them with these skills, you are empowering them to handle difficult situations and manage their emotions effectively.

In conclusion, promoting emotional intelligence and resilience in your child is vital for their overall well-being and success in life. By fostering open communication, allowing them to experience failure, and teaching problem-solving and coping skills, you are setting them up for a future where they can confidently navigate life's ups and downs. Remember, parenting with purpose means nurturing your child's potential by helping them develop the emotional intelligence and resilience they need to thrive.

Chapter 4: Nurturing Your Child's Physical Health

Providing Proper Nutrition and Healthy Eating Habits

As parents, one of the most crucial aspects of nurturing your child's potential is ensuring they receive proper nutrition and develop healthy eating habits. The food your child consumes plays a significant role in their physical growth, mental development, and overall well-being. In this subchapter, we will explore the importance of providing balanced meals, fostering a positive relationship with food, and offering practical tips to promote healthy eating habits.

A balanced diet is essential for your child's growth and development. It should include a variety of foods from different food groups, such as fruits, vegetables, whole grains, lean proteins, and dairy products. By offering a wide range of nutrients, you can support their immune system, enhance cognitive function, and maintain a healthy weight. Encourage your child to experiment with new flavors and textures and involve them in meal planning and preparation to instill a sense of ownership and excitement about healthy eating.

Fostering a positive relationship with food is crucial to avoid the development of unhealthy eating habits or disorders. Encourage your child to listen to their body's hunger and fullness cues, rather than relying on external factors or emotional triggers. Avoid labeling foods as "good" or "bad" but rather emphasize the importance of balance and moderation. Lead by example and demonstrate healthy eating habits yourself, as children often imitate their parent's behaviors.

Here are some practical tips to promote healthy eating habits in your child's daily life:

1. Stock your pantry and refrigerator with nutritious options: Fill your kitchen with fruits, vegetables, whole grains, and lean protein sources. Limit the presence of processed and sugary snacks to encourage healthier choices.

2. Make mealtimes a family affair: Eating together as a family promotes bonding and provides an opportunity to model healthy eating habits. Create a positive and relaxed environment where everyone can enjoy their meals and engage in meaningful conversations.

3. Encourage water consumption: Water is essential for hydration and aids in digestion. Limit sugary drinks and encourage your child to drink water throughout the day.

4. Limit screen time during meals: Distractions like television or mobile devices can hinder mindful eating. Encourage your child to focus on their food and engage in conversation during meals.

By prioritizing proper nutrition and cultivating healthy eating habits, you are nurturing your child's potential for a lifetime of good health. Providing a balanced diet and fostering a positive relationship with food will not only benefit their physical well-being but also contribute to their overall growth and development. Remember, your role as a parent is instrumental in shaping their understanding and appreciation of healthy eating habits.

Ensuring Sufficient Sleep and Rest

In the fast-paced and demanding world we live in, it is crucial for parents to prioritize their child's sleep and rest. Adequate sleep is not only essential for a child's physical and mental well-being, but it also plays a vital role in nurturing their potential. As parents, it is our responsibility to create an environment that promotes healthy sleep habits and ensures our children get the rest they need.

One of the primary reasons sleep is so crucial for children is its impact on their overall development. During sleep, their bodies grow and repair, while their brains process and consolidate information. Sufficient sleep helps enhance their memory, attention span, and cognitive abilities, which are vital for their learning and academic success. Additionally, sleep deprivation can lead to increased irritability, difficulty concentrating, and even behavioral problems in children.

To ensure your child enjoys sufficient sleep and rest, it is essential to establish a consistent bedtime routine. A routine helps signal to their bodies that it is time to wind down and prepare for sleep. Consider activities such as reading a book, taking a warm bath, or engaging in calming exercises like deep breathing or stretching. Avoid stimulating activities, such as screen time, close to bedtime, as they can interfere with your child's ability to fall asleep.

Creating a sleep-friendly environment is also crucial. Make sure your child's bedroom is cool, dark, and quiet. Invest in comfortable bedding and a supportive mattress that promotes healthy sleep posture. Limit exposure to electronic devices in the bedroom, as the blue light emitted by screens can disrupt the natural sleep-wake cycle.

Furthermore, be mindful of your child's sleep schedule. Age-appropriate sleep durations vary, and it is essential to ensure your child is getting the recommended amount for their age group. Avoid overscheduling activities or allowing excessive screen time, as it can lead to sleep deprivation. Encourage physical activity during the day, as exercise can promote better sleep at night.

Lastly, lead by example. As parents, it is crucial to prioritize our own sleep and rest. Modeling healthy sleep habits not only benefits our well-being but also demonstrates the importance of sleep to our children. Make a conscious effort to establish your own bedtime routine and create a sleep-friendly environment for yourself.

Remember, ensuring sufficient sleep and rest is an investment in your child's potential. By prioritizing their sleep needs, you are setting them up for success in various aspects of their life, from academic performance to emotional well-being. So, let us make a commitment to create a nurturing environment that fosters healthy sleep habits and supports our children's growth and development.

Encouraging Regular Physical Activity and Exercise

In today's fast-paced and technology-driven world, it's more important than ever to encourage regular physical activity and exercise in our children. As parents, we play a vital role in helping our kids develop healthy habits that will benefit them throughout their lives. Not only does regular physical activity help keep our children fit and active, but it also promotes overall well-being, boosts self-esteem, and improves cognitive function. In this subchapter, we will explore effective strategies to encourage physical activity and exercise in our children.

One of the first steps in encouraging regular physical activity is leading by example. Children often look up to their parents as role models, so it's essential for us to prioritize our own physical health and engage in regular exercise routines. By demonstrating the importance of staying active, we can inspire our children to follow suit. Whether it's going for family walks, biking together on weekends, or engaging in fun outdoor activities, spending quality time together while being physically active sets a positive example.

Another effective way to encourage physical activity is by making it enjoyable and fun. Children are more likely to engage in activities they find entertaining, so try to incorporate games, sports, or dance routines into their daily routine. Organize family sports tournaments or regular outings to the park, where they can explore different activities and make new friends. Additionally, involving children in choosing their preferred activities allows them to take ownership and feel motivated to participate.

Limiting screen time is crucial in promoting physical activity. Excessive screen time not only hinders children's physical development but also replaces valuable time that could be spent engaging in outdoor play or sports. Set reasonable limits on screen time and encourage alternative activities like swimming, biking, or playing team sports. By creating a balance between screen time and physical activity, we can ensure our children's overall well-being.

Lastly, praise and positive reinforcement can go a long way in motivating children to stay active. Recognize their efforts and achievements, whether it's completing a challenging hike, mastering a new sport, or consistently participating in physical activities. Positive reinforcement boosts their self-esteem and encourages them to continue being active.

In conclusion, as parents, it is our responsibility to encourage regular physical activity and exercise in our children. By leading by example, making it enjoyable, limiting screen time, and providing praise and positive reinforcement, we can help our children develop healthy habits that will benefit them throughout their lives. By nurturing their physical well-being, we are nurturing their potential.

Chapter 5: Cultivating Intellectual Growth

Creating a Stimulating Learning Environment

As parents, one of our primary responsibilities is to provide our children with a stimulating learning environment. A stimulating learning environment not only promotes a love for learning but also nurtures a child's potential. In this subchapter, we will explore various ways in which you can create such an environment for your child.

First and foremost, it is essential to create a space that is conducive to learning. This can be a dedicated study area or even a corner in their room. Ensure that the space is well-lit, organized, and free from distractions. A clutter-free environment promotes focus and concentration, allowing your child to make the most of their study time.

Another crucial aspect of a stimulating learning environment is the availability of resources. Stock up on age-appropriate books, educational toys, puzzles, and art supplies. Encourage your child to explore different subjects and interests by providing a variety of resources. A well-stocked bookshelf not only promotes reading but also exposes your child to different ideas and perspectives.

Technology can also play a significant role in creating a stimulating learning environment. With the advancements in technology, there are numerous educational apps, websites, and online courses available for children. However, it is crucial to strike a balance and ensure that screen time is limited and monitored. Encourage your child to use technology as a tool for learning rather than a source of entertainment.

In addition to the physical environment, it is equally important to foster a supportive and encouraging atmosphere at home. Celebrate your child's achievements, no matter how small, and provide constructive feedback. Encourage them to ask questions, explore their curiosity, and think critically. Create a safe space where mistakes are seen as opportunities for growth and learning.

Lastly, remember that learning doesn't only happen within the four walls of a classroom or at a desk. Take advantage of teachable moments in everyday life. Whether it's cooking together, exploring nature, or discussing current events, make learning a part of your daily routine. Engage in meaningful conversations and encourage your child to express their thoughts and opinions.

By creating a stimulating learning environment, you are nurturing your child's potential and setting them up for success. Remember, every child is unique, so adapt these suggestions to suit your child's individual needs and interests. With your guidance and support, your child will develop a lifelong love for learning and achieve their full potential.

Instilling a Love for Reading and Lifelong Learning

One of the greatest gifts you can give your child is a love for reading and a thirst for lifelong learning. In today's fast-paced world, where screens dominate our attention, fostering a love for books may seem like a daunting task. However, with some intentional efforts and a nurturing environment, you can cultivate a passion for reading in your child that will benefit them throughout their lives.

Reading opens up a world of imagination, knowledge, and empathy. It allows children to explore new places, experience different cultures, and understand diverse perspectives. As parents, it is our responsibility to create an environment that promotes reading and encourages curiosity.

Start by making reading a part of your daily routine. Set aside specific times for reading, whether it's before bedtime or during a cozy weekend afternoon. Make it a habit to read aloud to your child from a young age, even before they can understand the words. This helps them develop a love for storytelling and the rhythm of language.

Create a dedicated reading space in your home. It can be a cozy corner with a comfortable chair and a bookshelf filled with age-appropriate books. Make sure your child has easy access to a variety of books that cater to their interests and reading level. Visit libraries and bookstores together, allowing them to choose books that capture their attention.

Lead by example. Let your child see you reading regularly. Whether it's a novel, a newspaper, or a magazine, show them that reading is a pleasurable and valuable activity. Discuss books and articles you have read, and encourage them to share their thoughts and opinions.

Engage in meaningful conversations about books. Ask open-ended questions about the characters, plot, and themes. Encourage your child to think critically and form their own opinions. This not only enhances their reading comprehension skills but also fosters a love for intellectual discussions.

Utilize technology wisely. While screens can be distracting, they can also be powerful tools for encouraging reading. Explore educational apps and digital platforms that offer interactive reading experiences. However, set limits and ensure that screen time doesn't replace the joy of holding a physical book.

Lastly, celebrate milestones and achievements. When your child finishes a book or masters a new reading skill, acknowledge their efforts and reward them with praise or a special treat. This positive reinforcement will motivate them to continue exploring the world of literature.

By instilling a love for reading and lifelong learning, you are equipping your child with the tools to succeed academically and intellectually. More importantly, you are nurturing their imagination, empathy, and curiosity, which will benefit them in all aspects of life.

Supporting Educational Success and Academic Achievements

As parents, one of our greatest desires is to see our children succeed academically. We understand that education is the key to unlocking their potential and providing them with a bright future. In this subchapter, we will explore effective strategies to support your child's educational success and foster their academic achievements.

First and foremost, it is crucial to create a positive learning environment at home. Establish a designated study area that is free from distractions and equipped with necessary resources. Encourage regular study habits and establish a consistent routine, ensuring that they have ample time to complete their homework and revise their lessons. By providing them with a structured environment, you are setting the foundation for their academic growth.

Communication plays a vital role in supporting your child's educational journey. Regularly engage with their teachers and stay updated on their progress and challenges. Attend parent-teacher meetings and actively participate in school activities. By developing a strong relationship with their teachers, you can better understand your child's strengths and weaknesses, enabling you to provide targeted support.

In addition to open communication with teachers, it is essential to maintain an open line of communication with your child. Encourage them to share their thoughts, concerns, and aspirations regarding their education. Actively listen and provide guidance when needed. By fostering open communication, you are creating a safe space for them to express themselves and seek help when required.

Another key aspect of supporting your child's educational success is fostering a love for learning. Encourage their curiosity and provide opportunities for intellectual growth beyond the classroom. Take them to museums, libraries, and cultural events. Engage in discussions about current events and encourage them to explore various subjects of interest. By instilling a passion for learning, you are nurturing their intrinsic motivation, which is crucial for long-term academic success.

Lastly, it is important to recognize and celebrate your child's accomplishments, regardless of their scale. Praise their efforts, celebrate their achievements, and provide positive reinforcement. By acknowledging their hard work, you are boosting their self-esteem and motivation to excel academically.

In conclusion, supporting your child's educational success and academic achievements requires a holistic approach. By creating a positive learning environment, maintaining open communication, fostering a love for learning, and celebrating their accomplishments, you are providing the necessary support to nurture their potential. Remember, your involvement as a parent is instrumental in shaping their educational journey and unlocking their limitless possibilities.

Chapter 6: Nurturing Emotional Well-being

Teaching Emotional Awareness and Regulation

Emotional awareness and regulation are crucial skills that parents can teach their children. When children learn to identify and understand their emotions, they become better equipped to manage them effectively. This subchapter aims to guide parents in nurturing their child's emotional intelligence by teaching them emotional awareness and regulation.

Emotional awareness involves the ability to recognize and understand one's own emotions as well as the emotions of others. To develop this skill, parents can encourage open and honest communication with their children. By creating a safe and non-judgmental space, parents can foster an environment where children feel comfortable expressing their emotions. Engaging in conversations about feelings will help children develop a vocabulary to describe their emotions accurately.

Parents should also lead by example and demonstrate emotional awareness themselves. By openly discussing their own emotions and modeling healthy coping strategies, parents can show their children that it is normal and acceptable to feel a wide range of emotions. Additionally, parents can encourage their children to empathize with others by discussing how different situations might make others feel.

Once children have developed emotional awareness, the next step is teaching them how to regulate their emotions effectively. Emotion regulation involves managing emotions in a way that promotes healthy behavior and well-being. Parents can teach their children various self-regulation techniques, such as deep breathing exercises, mindfulness, and engaging in physical activities like sports or dancing.

It is important for parents to create a consistent routine that includes time for emotional regulation activities. By integrating these practices into their daily lives, children will learn to identify when they are experiencing intense emotions and develop strategies to calm themselves down.

Furthermore, parents can assist their children in problem-solving when they encounter challenging situations. By encouraging them to think critically and find solutions, parents empower their children to handle difficult emotions constructively. Teaching children to focus on finding resolutions rather than dwelling on the problem will enhance their emotional regulation skills.

Overall, teaching emotional awareness and regulation is a vital component of parenting with purpose. By developing these skills, children will be better equipped to navigate the complexities of their emotions and develop healthy relationships. Through open communication, leading by example, and providing opportunities for self-regulation, parents can nurture their child's emotional intelligence and support their overall well-being.

Building Strong Emotional Bonds and Attachment

In the journey of parenting, one of the most important aspects is building strong emotional bonds and attachment with your child. These bonds lay the foundation for a healthy and nurturing relationship, which can have a profound impact on your child's emotional well-being and overall development. This subchapter aims to guide parents on how to foster these strong emotional connections, emphasizing the significance of building a secure attachment with their child.

Attachment refers to the emotional bond that develops between a child and their primary caregiver, usually the parent. It begins during infancy and continues throughout childhood, shaping the child's ability to form relationships and navigate the world around them. Research has shown that children who have secure attachments with their parents tend to have higher self-esteem, better social skills, and improved emotional regulation.

So, how can parents build these strong emotional bonds and foster a secure attachment? Firstly, it is crucial to provide a warm and nurturing environment. This means being responsive to your child's needs, offering comfort and reassurance when they are upset, and showing genuine love and affection. Taking the time to engage in quality bonding activities, such as reading together or having regular family meals, can also strengthen the emotional connection between parent and child.

Additionally, practicing active listening is key to building strong emotional bonds. Listening attentively to your child's thoughts, feelings, and concerns demonstrates that their voice matters and that you genuinely care. Through active listening, parents can better understand their child's emotions and provide the necessary support and guidance.

Another essential component of building strong emotional bonds and attachments is establishing consistent and healthy routines. Predictable routines create a sense of security and stability for children, helping them feel safe and loved. Whether it's establishing a bedtime routine or having regular family rituals, these consistent practices foster a deep sense of belonging and attachment within the child.

Lastly, creating opportunities for open and honest communication is vital. Encouraging your child to express their feelings and thoughts without judgment allows them to trust and rely on you as a confidant. This open line of communication helps build a strong emotional bond and enables parents to better understand their child's needs, concerns, and aspirations.

In conclusion, building strong emotional bonds and attachment is a fundamental aspect of parenting. By providing a nurturing environment, practicing active listening, establishing consistent routines, and fostering open communication, parents can cultivate a secure attachment with their children. These emotional connections will not only enhance the parent-child relationship but also lay the groundwork for their child's emotional well-being and future relationships.

Addressing and Managing Stress and Anxiety

Parenting is a rewarding and fulfilling journey, but it can also be overwhelming and stressful at times. As parents, it is crucial to recognize and address our own stress and anxiety so that we can provide a nurturing and supportive environment for our children. In this subchapter, we will explore effective strategies for managing stress and anxiety while parenting with purpose.

First and foremost, it is important to acknowledge that stress and anxiety are normal emotions that everyone experiences. As parents, we often face numerous challenges, such as balancing work and family life, financial pressures, and the responsibility of raising our children. It is essential to remember that we are not alone in these feelings, and seeking support from other parents or professionals can be extremely helpful.

One effective technique for managing stress and anxiety is practicing self-care. Taking care of ourselves allows us to be the best parents we can be. This can include activities such as regular exercise, getting enough sleep, eating well, and engaging in hobbies or activities that bring us joy. By prioritizing our own well-being, we can better manage stress and model healthy coping mechanisms for our children.

Another valuable strategy is practicing mindfulness and relaxation techniques. Mindfulness involves being present in the moment and accepting our thoughts and feelings without judgment. This can be achieved through practices such as deep breathing exercises, meditation, or yoga. By incorporating mindfulness into our daily lives, we can reduce stress and increase our overall sense of well-being.

Additionally, effective time management is crucial in reducing stress and anxiety. As parents, our to-do lists can feel never-ending, which can lead to overwhelming feelings. By prioritizing tasks, setting realistic goals, and delegating responsibilities when possible, we can create a more balanced and manageable schedule. This allows us to focus on what truly matters and reduces feelings of being overwhelmed.

Lastly, fostering open and honest communication within our families is vital. Encouraging our children to express their emotions and concerns helps them develop healthy coping mechanisms for stress and anxiety. By creating a safe and supportive environment, we teach them that it is okay to seek help and support when needed.

In conclusion, addressing and managing stress and anxiety is crucial for parents in order to provide a nurturing and supportive environment for our children. By practicing self-care, mindfulness, effective time management, and fostering open communication, we can navigate the challenges of parenting with purpose. Remember, you are not alone in this journey, and seeking support is a sign of strength.

Chapter 7: Fostering Social Skills and Relationships

Developing Empathy and Compassion

As parents, one of our greatest responsibilities is to nurture our child's potential. We want to raise well-rounded individuals who are not only successful in their endeavors but also kind-hearted and compassionate human beings. Empathy and compassion are essential qualities that can positively impact our children's relationships, personal growth, and overall happiness. In this subchapter, we will explore effective strategies to help parents cultivate empathy and compassion in their children.

The first step in developing empathy and compassion is leading by example. Children learn best by observing their parents' behavior and attitudes. Therefore, it is important for parents to exhibit empathy and compassion in their daily interactions. Show your child understanding and patience when they make mistakes or face challenges. Teach them how to be compassionate by demonstrating acts of kindness towards others, whether it's volunteering together as a family or simply helping a neighbor in need.

Another valuable tool for developing empathy and compassion is encouraging open communication. Create a safe and non-judgmental environment where your child feels comfortable expressing their thoughts and emotions. Listen attentively to their concerns and validate their feelings. This will teach them the importance of empathy and understanding towards others' experiences.

Teaching empathy can also be done through storytelling. Choose books, movies, or even real-life stories that highlight acts of kindness, empathy, and compassion. Discuss these stories with your child, asking questions that encourage them to empathize with the characters and consider different perspectives. This will help them develop a broader worldview and a deeper understanding of others' feelings and experiences.

Additionally, practicing gratitude can play a significant role in fostering empathy and compassion. Encourage your child to reflect on the things they are grateful for and discuss how they can help those who may be less fortunate. Engage them in activities such as donating toys or clothes to those in need or participating in community service projects. By doing so, you are instilling a sense of empathy and compassion, as well as teaching the importance of giving back to the community.

In conclusion, developing empathy and compassion in our children is crucial for their personal growth and fulfilling relationships. By leading by example, encouraging open communication, using storytelling, and practicing gratitude, parents can help shape their children into empathetic and compassionate individuals. Remember, the journey towards empathy and compassion starts at home, and by nurturing these qualities in our children, we are not only shaping their future but also contributing to creating a more compassionate and empathetic society.

Teaching Effective Communication and Conflict Resolution

In today's fast-paced world, effective communication skills have become more crucial than ever. As parents, we play a vital role in nurturing our child's potential, and teaching them effective communication and conflict resolution skills is essential for their personal and social development. In this subchapter, we will explore various strategies and techniques to help parents navigate the challenging task of teaching these skills.

Effective communication is the foundation of healthy relationships. By modeling good communication ourselves, we can teach our children the importance of active listening, clear expression, and respectful dialogue. Encourage open and honest conversations at home, where everyone feels heard and valued. Teach your child to express their thoughts and emotions assertively, while also emphasizing the importance of empathy and understanding.

Conflict is an inevitable part of life, and learning how to resolve conflicts peacefully is a valuable skill. Teach your child to recognize and manage their emotions during conflicts. Encourage them to take a step back, breathe, and consider different perspectives before reacting impulsively. Teach them negotiation and problem-solving skills to help them find win-win solutions, rather than resorting to aggression or manipulation.

Role-playing is an effective technique to help children practice communication and conflict resolution skills. Create scenarios where your child can take different roles and practice expressing themselves respectfully, actively listening, and finding compromises. Provide constructive feedback and encourage them to reflect on their own communication style.

It is also important to teach children the art of effective non-verbal communication. Help them understand the impact of body language, facial expressions, and tone of voice on the way their message is received. Encourage them to be mindful of their non-verbal cues when interacting with others.

As parents, it is important to create a safe and supportive environment where children feel comfortable expressing their thoughts and concerns. Foster an atmosphere of trust and understanding, where conflicts are viewed as opportunities for growth and learning. Encourage your child to express their opinions, even if they differ from yours, and validate their feelings.

By teaching effective communication and conflict resolution skills, we equip our children with the tools they need to navigate the complexities of the world. These skills will not only benefit their personal relationships but also prepare them for success in their academic and professional lives. Remember, parenting with purpose means nurturing your child's potential to become confident, compassionate, and effective communicators.

Nurturing Healthy Friendships and Peer Interactions

As parents, we play a vital role in shaping and guiding our children's social development. One of the most important aspects of their social lives is forming healthy friendships and engaging in positive peer interactions. In this subchapter, we will explore the significance of nurturing these relationships and provide practical tips to help parents navigate this essential aspect of parenting.

Healthy friendships are crucial for a child's emotional and social well-being. They provide support, companionship, and a sense of belonging. By fostering positive peer interactions, we can help our children develop important social skills, empathy, and conflict resolution abilities.

First and foremost, it is essential to encourage open communication with our children about their friendships. By actively listening to their experiences, concerns, and joys, we create a safe space for them to share and seek guidance. Regular conversations about friendships can help us identify any potential issues or challenges, allowing us to provide the necessary support.

Teaching our children empathy is another crucial aspect of nurturing healthy friendships. Empathy allows them to understand and share the feelings of others, promoting kindness and compassion. Encourage your child to put themselves in their friend's shoes, helping them develop a deeper understanding of different perspectives.

Additionally, setting clear boundaries and teaching conflict resolution skills is paramount. Children need to understand the importance of respecting personal space, opinions, and choices. Teach them effective communication techniques, such as active listening and expressing their feelings assertively, to resolve conflicts peacefully.

Encouraging our children to participate in group activities and clubs can also promote healthy peer interactions. These settings provide opportunities for them to socialize, collaborate, and build lasting friendships based on common interests and shared experiences.

It is equally important for parents to model healthy friendships in their own lives. Our children observe and learn from our behavior, so it is crucial to demonstrate positive communication, empathy, and conflict resolution skills in our own friendships. By being good role models, we instill these values in our children, helping them develop healthy and nurturing relationships.

In conclusion, nurturing healthy friendships and peer interactions is an essential part of parenting. By actively engaging with our children, teaching empathy and conflict resolution skills, encouraging participation in group activities, and modeling healthy friendships ourselves, we can build a solid foundation for their social development. Remember, fostering healthy friendships is not just about the present; it equips our children with lifelong skills that will benefit them in all aspects of their lives.

Chapter 8: Encouraging Creativity and Imagination

Providing Opportunities for Artistic Expression

Artistic expression is a vital aspect of a child's development, fostering creativity, imagination, and emotional intelligence. As parents, it is essential to provide ample opportunities for our children to explore and express their artistic abilities. This subchapter will guide you on how to create an environment that nurtures your child's artistic potential.

Encourage Creative Play: From a young age, children engage in imaginative play, which serves as a foundation for artistic expression. Encourage your child to create stories, build with blocks, or engage in role-playing. These activities help develop their creativity and problem-solving skills.

Expose Them to Various Art Forms: Introduce your child to different forms of art such as painting, drawing, music, dance, and theater. Attend local art exhibitions, concerts, or performances together. Exposing them to diverse art forms broadens their horizons and allows them to find their artistic niche.

Provide Art Supplies: Set up an art corner or a designated space where your child can freely experiment with various art supplies. Offer a wide range of materials such as paints, crayons, markers, colored pencils, clay, and collage materials. Allowing them to explore different mediums will enhance their artistic skills and encourage self-expression.

Support their Passion: Pay attention to your child's interests and encourage their passion for a specific art form. If they show a keen interest in painting, enroll them in an art class or provide additional resources and materials to nurture their talent. Supporting their passion will boost their confidence and motivation to pursue their artistic endeavors.

Celebrate Their Artwork: Display your child's artwork throughout your home. Celebrate their creative achievements by framing their paintings or creating a dedicated gallery wall. This not only boosts their self-esteem but also reinforces the importance of artistic expression in your family.

Incorporate Art into Daily Life: Encourage your child to find artistic inspiration in everyday life. Take nature walks, visit museums, or explore the city's street art scene. Engaging with art in real-world settings helps them develop a keen eye for beauty and creativity.

Collaborative Projects: Encourage your child to engage in collaborative art projects with their siblings or friends. This fosters teamwork, communication, and the ability to appreciate different perspectives.

Remember, the goal is not to create the next Picasso but to provide an environment where your child feels supported and encouraged to express themselves artistically. By providing opportunities for artistic expression, you are nurturing your child's potential and helping them develop into well-rounded individuals with a deep appreciation for the arts.

Supporting Curiosity and Problem-Solving Skills

As parents, one of our greatest responsibilities is to nurture our child's potential. We want them to grow into confident, independent individuals who can think critically and come up with innovative solutions to life's challenges. Cultivating curiosity and problem-solving skills is an essential part of this process.

Curiosity is the driving force behind learning and discovery. It fuels a child's desire to explore, ask questions, and seek answers. Encouraging curiosity can be as simple as providing a safe and stimulating environment that sparks their interest. Surround your child with age-appropriate books, toys, and games that encourage exploration and hands-on learning. Take the time to engage in meaningful conversations, listen to their ideas, and support their interests. By showing genuine interest in their curiosity, you are validating their thoughts and encouraging them to continue exploring.

Problem-solving skills are essential for navigating life's challenges. As parents, we can foster these skills by allowing our children to face and overcome obstacles. Resist the urge to immediately solve problems for them. Instead, guide them through the process, asking open-ended questions that encourage critical thinking. Teach them to break down complex problems into smaller, manageable tasks. By doing so, you empower them to develop their problem-solving abilities and build resilience.

Modeling problem-solving skills is equally important. Let your children observe you as you face challenges and find solutions. Discuss your thinking process out loud, emphasizing the importance of perseverance and creative thinking. This will not only teach them problem-solving skills but also instill the value of learning from mistakes and embracing challenges.

Encourage your child to engage in activities that stimulate problem-solving, such as puzzles, building blocks, or even coding. These activities promote logical thinking, spatial awareness, and creativity. Additionally, consider introducing them to real-world problems and involve them in brainstorming solutions. This will help them understand the significance of their problem-solving skills and inspire them to make a positive impact on the world around them.

Remember, supporting curiosity and problem-solving skills is an ongoing process. It requires patience, encouragement, and an open mind. By nurturing these skills in your child, you are setting them up for a lifetime of learning, growth, and success.

Embracing and Celebrating Individuality

In a world that often values conformity, it is essential for parents to embrace and celebrate their child's individuality. As parents, our primary goal should be to nurture our children's potential and help them grow into confident and authentic individuals. Understanding and appreciating their uniqueness will not only strengthen the parent-child bond but also provide a solid foundation for their future success.

Every child is born with their own set of talents, interests, and personality traits. It is our responsibility as parents to recognize and encourage these individual qualities. By doing so, we can help our children develop a strong sense of self and the confidence to pursue their passions. Instead of molding them into our own image or societal expectations, we should create a safe and supportive environment in which they can explore their own identity.

To embrace and celebrate individuality, it is important to foster open and honest communication with our children. By actively listening and engaging in meaningful conversations, we can gain insights into their thoughts, dreams, and aspirations. This will not only help us understand their unique perspective but also enable us to provide guidance and support tailored to their needs.

Furthermore, it is crucial to expose our children to diverse experiences and opportunities. Encouraging them to explore different hobbies, interests, and cultures will broaden their horizons and allow them to discover their true passions. By exposing them to a variety of experiences, we can help them develop a strong sense of empathy, respect, and acceptance towards others, regardless of their differences.

As parents, we must also be mindful of our own biases and expectations. It is essential to avoid projecting our own unfulfilled dreams onto our children. Instead, we should focus on their strengths, talents, and unique abilities. By setting realistic expectations and nurturing their individuality, we can empower them to reach their full potential and lead meaningful lives.

In conclusion, embracing and celebrating individuality is a fundamental aspect of parenting with purpose. By creating an environment that values and encourages their uniqueness, we can help our children develop a strong sense of self and pursue their passions. Through open communication, exposure to diverse experiences, and a mindful approach, we can raise confident, authentic, and successful individuals who will positively impact the world around them.

Chapter 9: Parenting Through Different Stages of Childhood

Parenting Strategies for the Infant and Toddler Years

The infant and toddler years are a crucial period in a child's development. During this time, parents have the opportunity to lay the foundation for their child's future growth and potential. In this subchapter, we will explore effective parenting strategies that can help parents navigate this exciting yet challenging phase of their child's life.

1. Establishing routines: Infants and toddlers thrive on predictability and consistency. By establishing daily routines for activities like feeding, sleeping, and playtime, parents can create a sense of security and stability for their children. Consistent routines also promote healthy habits and help children feel more in control of their environment.

2. Responsive parenting: Infants and toddlers rely on their parents for guidance and support. Being responsive to their needs, whether it's a hungry cry or a desire for comfort, helps build a strong parent-child bond. Responding promptly and attentively to their cues fosters trust and promotes healthy emotional development.

3. Encouraging exploration and independence: As infants grow into toddlers, they become more curious and eager to explore the world around them. Parents

should create a safe and stimulating environment that encourages their child's natural curiosity. Allowing them to explore their surroundings independently, with appropriate supervision, helps build confidence and self-esteem.

4. Positive discipline: It's important to set age-appropriate boundaries and provide consistent discipline during the infant and toddler years. Rather than resorting to harsh punishment, parents should focus on positive reinforcement and redirection. Praising good behavior and using gentle reminders help toddlers understand expectations and develop self-control.

5. Building a strong support system: Parenting can be challenging, especially during the early years. It's essential for parents to seek support from family, friends, and parenting communities. Connecting with other parents can provide valuable advice, reassurance, and a sense of belonging.

6. Self-care for parents: Taking care of oneself is equally important as caring for a child. Parents need to prioritize their physical and mental well-being to be effective caregivers. Finding time for relaxation, exercise, and pursuing personal interests helps parents recharge and maintain a positive mindset.

7. Cultivating a love for learning: Even during the infant and toddler years, children are constantly learning and absorbing information. Parents can foster

a love for learning by engaging in age-appropriate activities that stimulate their child's senses and promote cognitive development. Reading books, singing songs, and engaging in sensory play are all excellent ways to nurture a child's curiosity and thirst for knowledge.

In conclusion, the infant and toddler years are a critical time for parents to lay the groundwork for their child's future development. By implementing these effective parenting strategies, parents can provide a nurturing and supportive environment that fosters their child's potential.

Navigating the Challenges of the School-Age Years

The school-age years can be an exciting and challenging time for both parents and children. As your child grows and enters elementary school, they will face new experiences, expectations, and social dynamics. It is during this phase that parents play a crucial role in nurturing their child's potential and helping them navigate the challenges that lie ahead.

One of the key challenges parents face during the school age years is finding a balance between supporting their child's independence and providing guidance. As children become more autonomous, it is important for parents to encourage their decision-making skills while still offering guidance and setting boundaries. This delicate balance helps children develop a sense of responsibility and self-confidence.

Academic pressures can also become more prominent during this time. As your child progresses through elementary school, they may encounter challenges in their studies or struggle with organizational skills. As a parent, it is essential to create a supportive and structured environment that encourages learning and growth. This may involve establishing a consistent homework routine, setting realistic expectations, and providing resources or tutoring when necessary.

Social development is another crucial aspect of the school-age years. Your child will form friendships, navigate group dynamics, and learn how to communicate effectively. As a parent, it is important to foster healthy social skills by encouraging empathy, listening, and conflict resolution. Helping your child develop strong social skills will empower them to form positive relationships and navigate any social challenges they may encounter.

Emotional development is also significant during the school-age years. Children may experience a range of emotions as they face new situations and navigate social interactions. As a parent, it is important to create a safe and supportive environment where your child feels comfortable expressing their feelings. Teaching emotional intelligence, such as identifying and managing emotions, will equip your child with valuable skills to navigate the ups and downs of their school years.

Overall, parenting during the school-age years requires adaptability, patience, and a nurturing approach. By balancing independence and guidance, providing academic support, fostering healthy social skills, and nurturing emotional development, parents can help their children navigate the challenges of this crucial phase. Embracing these challenges with purpose and intention will enable parents to support their child's growth and nurture their full potential.

Supporting Your Teenager's Transition to Adulthood

As parents, we play a crucial role in guiding our teenagers through the challenging and exciting phase of transitioning into adulthood. This subchapter aims to provide you with valuable insights and practical tips on how to support your teenager during this transformative period.

1. Open communication: Establishing an open and honest line of communication with your teenager is vital. Encourage them to express their feelings, concerns, and aspirations. Listen attentively without judgment, allowing them to voice their opinions and ideas freely. This will help build trust and strengthen your relationship.

2. Encourage independence: Adolescence is a time for teenagers to develop their independence and decision-making skills. Encourage them to take on responsibilities and make their own choices, while providing guidance and support when needed. This will empower them to become self-reliant and confident adults.

3. Foster self-discovery: Encourage your teenager to explore their interests and passions. Help them identify their strengths and talents, and guide them towards activities or hobbies that align with their aspirations. This will aid in their personal growth and provide a sense of direction as they move towards adulthood.

4. Teach financial literacy: Financial responsibility is an essential skill for adulthood. Introduce your teenager to the basics of budgeting, saving, and managing money. Teach them about the importance of financial planning and the consequences of overspending. This knowledge will lay a solid foundation for their future financial well-being.

5. Career guidance: Support your teenager in discovering their career interests and aspirations. Help them explore different career paths and provide information about various industries. Encourage internships, part-time jobs, or volunteering opportunities to gain practical experience. Guide them in making informed decisions about their educational and career choices.

6. Emotional well-being: Adolescence can be an emotionally turbulent time. Encourage your teenager to prioritize their mental health and well-being. Teach them effective coping mechanisms, such as practicing mindfulness, engaging in physical activity, or seeking professional help when needed. Provide a safe space for them to express their emotions and validate their experiences.

7. Encourage responsible decision-making: As teenagers begin to navigate the complexities of adulthood, it is crucial to teach them about responsible decision-making. Discuss the importance of considering the potential consequences of their actions

and making choices aligned with their values and goals.

By implementing these strategies, you can support your teenager's smooth transition into adulthood. Remember, parenting with purpose means nurturing your child's potential and guiding them toward a successful and fulfilling future.

Chapter 10: Balancing Parenting with Self-Care

Recognizing the Importance of Self-Care for Parents

As parents, we often find ourselves caught up in the whirlwind of daily responsibilities and demands. We prioritize our children's needs, ensuring they receive the best care, education, and opportunities. In the midst of this constant juggling act, it is easy to overlook the importance of self-care. However, recognizing and prioritizing our own self-care is vital for our well-being, our ability to parent effectively, and ultimately, for our children's overall development.

Parenting requires an incredible amount of physical, mental, and emotional energy. Neglecting our own needs can lead to burnout, increased stress levels, and ultimately impact our ability to be present and engaged parents. Self-care is not selfish; it is an essential component of effective parenting. When we prioritize our own well-being, we become better equipped to meet the challenges of parenting with grace and patience.

Taking time for self-care allows us to recharge and replenish our energy reserves. It can be as simple as carving out a few minutes each day for relaxation, engaging in a hobby, or enjoying a moment of solitude. By engaging in activities that bring us joy and fulfillment, we are better able to model healthy behaviors for our children. They learn the importance of self-care by witnessing us prioritize our own well-being.

Self-care is not limited to physical activities; it encompasses our mental and emotional well-being as well. It is important to acknowledge and address our own emotional needs, seeking support and guidance when necessary. Connecting with other parents, joining a support group, or seeking professional help can provide valuable insight, reassurance, and coping strategies.

By recognizing the importance of self-care, we also teach our children the value of self-love and self-worth. As parents, we play a vital role in shaping our children's perceptions of themselves and their own self-care practices. When they witness us prioritizing our well-being, they learn that self-care is not only important but also necessary for leading a balanced and fulfilling life.

In conclusion, recognizing the importance of self-care for parents is essential for our own well-being and our ability to parent effectively. Prioritizing self-care allows us to recharge, model healthy behaviors, and teach our children the value of self-love and self-worth. By nurturing ourselves, we create an environment where our children can thrive, knowing that their parents are taking care of themselves in order to be the best parents they can be. So, let us make a conscious effort to prioritize our own self-care, for the sake of our own well-being and the future of our children.

Strategies for Managing Parental Stress and Burnout

Parenting is undoubtedly one of the most rewarding experiences in life. However, it can also be incredibly challenging and overwhelming, leading to parental stress and burnout. As parents, it is crucial to prioritize self-care and develop strategies to manage these feelings effectively. This subchapter will explore various strategies for managing parental stress and burnout, helping parents maintain their well-being while nurturing their child's potential.

1. Prioritize self-care: Remember that you cannot pour from an empty cup. Make self-care a priority by setting aside time for activities that rejuvenate you. Whether it's reading a book, taking a walk, or practicing meditation, finding moments of solitude can help you recharge and reduce stress.

2. Seek support: Don't hesitate to lean on your support system. Reach out to family, friends, or other parents who can provide guidance, empathy, and a listening ear. Join parenting support groups or online communities where you can share experiences and gain valuable insights.

3. Practice stress management techniques: Explore different stress management techniques such as deep breathing exercises, yoga, or mindfulness meditation. These practices can help you stay calm and centered amidst the challenges of parenting.

4. Set realistic expectations: It's essential to set realistic expectations for yourself as a parent. Remember that nobody is perfect, and it's okay to make mistakes. Understand that parenting is a learning process, and it's natural to feel overwhelmed at times. Be gentle with yourself and celebrate small victories along the way.

5. Delegate and share responsibilities: Don't be afraid to delegate tasks and share responsibilities with your partner or other family members. Sharing the load can alleviate stress and allow you to have more time for yourself and your child.

6. Take breaks: It's crucial to take regular breaks from parenting duties. Arrange for occasional childcare or engage your partner in taking over for a few hours. Use this time to recharge and engage in activities that bring you joy.

7. Maintain a healthy lifestyle: A healthy lifestyle is key to managing stress and burnout. Ensure you prioritize sleep, eat well-balanced meals, and engage in regular physical activity. Taking care of your physical well-being will positively impact your mental and emotional well-being as a parent.

By implementing these strategies, parents can effectively manage stress and burnout, creating a healthy and nurturing environment for their child's growth. Remember, taking care of yourself is not selfish but rather essential for being the best parent you can be.

Finding Joy and Fulfillment in Parenthood

Parenthood is a journey filled with ups and downs, but it is also one of the most rewarding experiences in life. As parents, we have the incredible opportunity to nurture and shape our child's potential, and in doing so, we find joy and fulfillment. In this subchapter, we will explore the ways in which we can discover and embrace the immense happiness that parenthood can bring.

First and foremost, it is essential to cultivate a positive mindset. Parenting can be challenging, but approaching it with optimism and an open heart can make all the difference. Embrace the small victories and let go of perfectionism. Remember that mistakes are an inevitable part of the process, and they offer valuable lessons for both you and your child.

Another key aspect of finding joy in parenthood is fostering a strong bond with your child. Take the time to connect with them on a deep level, engaging in meaningful conversations and activities. Show them that they are loved unconditionally and create a safe and nurturing environment where they can thrive. When you witness their growth and development, a sense of fulfillment will naturally arise.

Parenthood can sometimes feel overwhelming, and it is crucial to prioritize self-care. Taking care of yourself allows you to be the best parent you can be. Make time for activities that bring you joy and recharge your energy. Remember that you deserve happiness and fulfillment in your own life as well.

Furthermore, finding joy in parenthood means embracing the present moment. It is easy to get caught up in the worries and stress of the future or dwell on past mistakes. However, the true joy lies in treasuring the precious moments with your child and cherishing the memories you create together. Be fully present during bedtime stories, family dinners, and playtime – these simple moments are the ones that will bring you the most joy and fulfillment.

Lastly, seek support from fellow parents and parenting communities. Surrounding yourself with like-minded individuals who understand the challenges and joys of parenthood can be immensely comforting. Share your experiences, seek advice, and offer support to others. Remember, no one has all the answers, and by supporting each other, we can navigate the journey of parenthood with greater ease and joy.

In conclusion, finding joy and fulfillment in parenthood is a conscious choice that requires a positive mindset, a strong bond with your child, self-care, being present in the moment, and seeking support. Embrace the beauty of this incredible journey, and you will discover that parenthood has the power to bring immense joy and fulfillment to your life.

Chapter 11: Nurturing Your Child's Potential: Case Studies

Case Study 1: Overcoming Academic Challenges

Subchapter: Case Study 1: Overcoming Academic Challenges

Introduction:
In this subchapter, we will delve into an inspiring case study that highlights the importance of overcoming academic challenges for our children. Academic hurdles are a common part of a child's educational journey, and as parents, it is crucial to provide guidance and support to help them navigate these obstacles successfully. Through this case study, we aim to demonstrate effective strategies that can be employed to nurture your child's potential and ensure their academic growth.

Case   Study:
Meet Sarah, a bright and enthusiastic 10-year-old girl, who faced a significant academic challenge when she entered the fifth grade. Sarah had always been a diligent student, but suddenly she started struggling with math concepts, resulting in a decline in her grades. Concerned, Sarah's parents decided to take proactive steps to help her overcome this obstacle.

Identifying   the   Challenge:
Sarah's parents initiated open and honest communication with her, encouraging her to share her

feelings and concerns about math. They discovered that Sarah was experiencing anxiety and a lack of confidence due to the pressure she felt to perform well. Understanding the root cause of the challenge was crucial for devising an effective plan to support her.

Developing a Support System: Sarah's parents decided to establish a support system consisting of her teachers, a tutor, and themselves. They collaborated with Sarah's math teacher to identify specific areas where she was struggling and developed an individualized plan to address those gaps. Additionally, they enlisted the help of a skilled tutor who could provide personalized attention and guidance.

Building Confidence and Motivation: Recognizing that Sarah's confidence had taken a hit, her parents took proactive steps to rebuild it. They celebrated small victories, provided constant encouragement, and emphasized that mistakes were a natural part of the learning process. Sarah's parents also encouraged her to set realistic goals, helping her stay motivated throughout her academic journey.

Creating a Positive Learning Environment: To foster a positive learning environment at home, Sarah's parents created a dedicated study area, free from distractions. They set a consistent schedule for homework and encouraged regular study breaks. By implementing these strategies, Sarah developed a sense of discipline and focus, which ultimately aided in her academic success.

Results and Reflection:
With consistent effort and support, Sarah gradually regained her confidence and improved her math skills. Her grades began to improve, and she regained her enthusiasm for learning. The experience taught Sarah resilience, problem-solving skills, and the importance of seeking help when needed.

Conclusion:
Sarah's case study demonstrates the significance of parental involvement, open communication, and proactive measures in helping children overcome academic challenges. As parents, it is crucial to identify and address these hurdles early on, providing the necessary support, and fostering a positive learning environment. By nurturing our children's potential and instilling a growth mindset, we empower them to overcome obstacles and achieve academic success.

Case Study 2: Building Emotional Resilience

In today's fast-paced and unpredictable world, it has become increasingly important for parents to equip their children with emotional resilience. Emotional resilience is the ability to adapt and bounce back from challenging situations, setbacks, and adversity. As parents, we have a vital role to play in nurturing this essential life skill in our children.

Meet Sam and Emily, two siblings who have faced their fair share of emotional challenges. Sam, an introverted and shy child, often struggled with expressing his emotions and found it difficult to cope with social interactions. On the other hand, Emily, an outgoing and spirited child, had a tendency to get overwhelmed easily and would become easily upset when things didn't go her way.

Recognizing the need to build emotional resilience in their children, Sam and Emily's parents embarked on a journey to provide them with the necessary tools and support. They understood that resilience is not about shielding children from adversity but rather about teaching them how to navigate through it.

The first step was to create a safe and nurturing environment at home, where both Sam and Emily felt comfortable expressing their emotions. Their parents encouraged open communication and actively listened to their concerns without judgment. By doing so, they helped their children develop a sense of trust and security, allowing them to share their feelings more freely.

Next, Sam and Emily's parents introduced them to mindfulness and relaxation techniques. They learned how to manage their emotions by focusing on their breath, engaging in calming activities like drawing or listening to music, and practicing positive self-talk. These techniques provided them with a sense of control and helped them regulate their emotions during challenging moments.

Furthermore, Sam and Emily's parents encouraged them to embrace failures and setbacks as learning opportunities. They reframed these experiences as valuable lessons rather than something to be ashamed of. By doing so, they instilled in their children the belief that mistakes are a natural part of growth and that resilience is about bouncing back stronger.

Over time, Sam and Emily began to exhibit remarkable emotional resilience. Sam became more confident in expressing himself and developed better social skills. Emily learned to adapt to unexpected changes and became more flexible in dealing with disappointments.

The case study of Sam and Emily demonstrates the power of building emotional resilience in children. By providing a nurturing environment, teaching coping strategies, and reframing adversity, parents can equip their children with the skills to face life's challenges with strength and determination. Remember, building emotional resilience is a lifelong journey, and as parents, we play a crucial role in guiding our children towards emotional well-being and success.

Case Study 3: Cultivating a Passion for the Arts

Introduction:

In today's fast-paced world, parents are often concerned about their child's future success. While academic achievements and extracurricular activities like sports are prioritized, it is equally important to explore and cultivate a passion for the arts. In this case study, we will delve into the inspiring journey of the Johnson family, who successfully nurtured their child's love for the arts and witnessed the incredible impact it had on their child's overall development.

Background:

The Johnsons, a loving and supportive family, noticed their child, Emily, had a natural inclination towards artistic activities from a young age. Whether it was drawing, painting, or creating music, Emily found joy and expressed herself through artistic endeavors. Recognizing the importance of nurturing this passion, the Johnsons decided to provide Emily with ample opportunities to explore and grow in the arts.

Encouraging Exploration:

The Johnsons started by enrolling Emily in art classes and music lessons. They encouraged her to experiment with various art forms, giving her the freedom to express her creativity without judgment. This allowed Emily to develop her own artistic style and build confidence in her abilities.

Exposure to the Arts:

To further cultivate Emily's passion, the Johnsons exposed her to different forms of art. They took her to art galleries, museums, and live performances, exposing her to the works of renowned artists. This exposure not only broadened Emily's artistic horizons but also inspired her to dream big and set higher goals for herself.

Supporting and Nurturing:

Recognizing the importance of consistent support, the Johnsons created a nurturing environment at home. They provided Emily with the necessary art supplies, a designated space to create, and dedicated time for arts-related activities. Additionally, they praised her efforts and celebrated her achievements, fostering a sense of pride and motivation within Emily.

The Impact:

As Emily continued to delve deeper into the arts, her passion blossomed. Not only did she excel in her artistic endeavors, but she also experienced numerous benefits in other areas of her life. Her creativity and imagination flourished, leading to enhanced problem-solving skills and out-of-the-box thinking. Furthermore, her self-expression through art boosted her self-confidence and improved her communication abilities.

Conclusion:

The Johnsons' journey with Emily serves as an inspiring example of how nurturing a child's passion for the arts can unlock their full potential. By encouraging exploration, providing exposure, and offering unwavering support, parents can cultivate a lifelong love for the arts while simultaneously enriching their child's overall development. As parents, it is our responsibility to recognize and nurture our children's unique talents, ensuring they have the tools they need to succeed in all aspects of life.

Chapter 12: Embracing Parenthood with Purpose

Celebrating the Journey of Parenting

Parenting is a remarkable journey filled with ups and downs, triumphs and challenges. It is a journey that requires love, patience, and purpose. In this subchapter, "Celebrating the Journey of Parenting," we will explore the joys and rewards of being a parent, as well as the importance of cherishing every moment and nurturing your child's potential.

Parenting is not just about raising a child; it is about nurturing them to become the best version of themselves. As parents, we are responsible for providing a loving and supportive environment that allows our children to thrive. It is through this journey that we witness their growth, achievements, and milestones, and it is in these moments that we celebrate.

One of the greatest joys of parenting is seeing your child's smiling face and hearing their laughter. Every milestone, from their first step to their first word, fills our hearts with pride and joy. These moments are not only a celebration of their achievements but also a reminder of the incredible bond we share with our children.

While parenting can be challenging at times, it is important to remember that every obstacle is an opportunity for growth. As parents, we learn to be patient, understanding, and resilient. We celebrate our ability to overcome challenges together with our children, teaching them valuable life lessons along the way.

It is also crucial to celebrate the small victories in parenting. Whether it is a good grade at school, a kind gesture towards a friend, or a loving act towards a sibling, these accomplishments deserve recognition. Celebrating these moments not only boosts our child's self-esteem but also reinforces positive behavior and encourages them to continue growing.

In this subchapter, we will explore different ways to celebrate the journey of parenting. We will discuss the importance of quality time, creating family traditions, and finding joy in everyday moments. We will also explore the significance of self-care for parents, as taking care of ourselves allows us to be the best version of ourselves for our children.

Parenting with purpose is about embracing the journey and celebrating every step along the way. It is about nurturing our children's potential and helping them discover their passions and talents. So, let's embark on this incredible journey together and celebrate the joys of parenting, for it is in these moments that we truly find fulfillment.

Embracing Imperfections and Learning from Mistakes

As parents, we often strive for perfection in everything we do, constantly seeking to provide the best for our children. However, it is crucial to understand that perfection is an unattainable goal, and our imperfections can actually serve as valuable lessons for both us and our children. In this subchapter, we will explore the importance of embracing imperfections and learning from mistakes in our journey as parents.

It is natural to make mistakes as parents. We may lose our temper, make the wrong decision, or simply feel overwhelmed at times. It is essential not to dwell on these mistakes but rather view them as opportunities for growth. By acknowledging our imperfections and taking responsibility for our actions, we teach our children the valuable lesson of accountability. They learn that making mistakes is a part of life and that it is how we handle them that truly matters.

Moreover, when we embrace our imperfections, we create a safe and non-judgmental environment for our children. They, too, will make mistakes and face challenges throughout their lives. By showing them that it is okay to make mistakes, we encourage them to take risks, learn from their failures, and grow into resilient individuals.

Learning from our mistakes also allows us to model effective problem-solving skills for our children. When they see us analyzing our actions, reflecting on what went wrong, and making efforts to rectify the situation, they learn the importance of critical thinking and self-improvement. This mindset will serve them well in their own lives, enabling them to face challenges head-on and find creative solutions.

Furthermore, embracing imperfections fosters a growth mindset within our children. Instead of fearing failure, they will understand that mistakes are stepping stones towards success. They will be more willing to take on new challenges, push their limits, and persist in the face of adversity. This mindset nurtures their potential and encourages them to explore their passions without the fear of making mistakes.

In conclusion, embracing imperfections and learning from mistakes is an essential aspect of parenting with purpose. By modeling accountability, creating a non-judgmental environment, teaching problem-solving skills, and fostering a growth mindset, we empower our children to embrace their own imperfections and grow into resilient individuals. Remember, it is through our mistakes that we truly learn and evolve as parents and human beings.

Leaving a Lasting Legacy for Your Child

As parents, we all dream of leaving a lasting legacy for our children. We want to provide them with the tools and values they need to succeed in life and make a positive impact on the world. In this subchapter, we will explore the importance of creating a meaningful legacy and how we can do so through purposeful parenting.

First and foremost, it is essential to understand that a legacy is not about material possessions or wealth. Instead, it is about the values, principles, and lessons we impart to our children. It is about instilling in them a strong sense of character, empathy, and resilience. By focusing on these aspects, we can ensure that our children are equipped with the necessary skills to navigate life's challenges and contribute meaningfully to society.

One of the most powerful ways to leave a lasting legacy is through leading by example. Our children learn more from what they see us do than what we tell them to do. By embodying the values we want them to embrace, such as honesty, compassion, and integrity, we provide them with a solid foundation for their own moral development.

Another crucial aspect of leaving a legacy is fostering a love for learning and personal growth in our children. Encourage their curiosity, support their educational pursuits, and expose them to a wide range of experiences. By nurturing their potential, we empower them to pursue their dreams and make a difference in the world.

Communication plays a vital role in leaving a lasting legacy. Make time for meaningful conversations with your children, truly listening to their thoughts and feelings. Create a safe space where they feel comfortable expressing themselves and discussing important topics. By fostering open and honest communication, you foster trust and understanding, ensuring that your values and wisdom are passed down through generations.

Lastly, it is essential to teach our children the importance of giving back to others. Encourage them to engage in acts of kindness and volunteer in their community. By showing them the value of empathy and compassion, we empower them to make a positive impact on the lives of others.

Leaving a lasting legacy for your child is an ongoing process that requires dedication and intentionality. By focusing on instilling strong values, fostering personal growth, promoting open communication, and encouraging acts of kindness, you can ensure that your child's potential is nurtured and that they leave their mark on the world. Remember, the greatest legacy we can leave behind is the impact we have on our children's lives.

Conclusion:

Empowering Parents to Nurture Their Child's Potential

In today's fast-paced and ever-evolving world, parenting has become more challenging than ever before. As parents, we constantly strive to provide the best opportunities and guidance for our children, hoping to nurture their potential and help them succeed in life. It is within this context that empowering parents becomes crucial in shaping the future of our children.

Throughout this book, "Parenting with Purpose: Nurturing Your Child's Potential," we have explored various aspects of parenting from understanding child development to effective communication strategies. We have delved into the importance of setting boundaries, encouraging independence, and fostering a positive mindset. Now, as we conclude our journey together, we want to emphasize the significance of empowering parents to truly unlock their child's potential.

Empowerment begins with knowledge and understanding. As parents, we must continuously educate ourselves about child development, psychology, and the latest research in the field of parenting. Armed with this knowledge, we can make informed decisions, adapt our parenting styles, and provide an environment that supports our child's growth and development.

Moreover, empowering parents means encouraging self-reflection and self-awareness. It is essential to recognize our own strengths and weaknesses, acknowledging that we are not perfect. By cultivating a mindset of continuous learning and personal growth, we become better equipped to guide and nurture our children effectively.

One crucial aspect of empowerment is fostering a strong parent-child bond. Through open and honest communication, we can establish trust and create a safe space for our children to share their thoughts, feelings, and aspirations. By actively listening, offering support, and respecting their individuality, we can help them discover and pursue their passions.

Empowering parents also involves creating a supportive network of like-minded individuals. Joining parenting communities, attending workshops, and seeking guidance from professionals can provide valuable insights, reassurance, and a sense of belonging. It is through these connections that we gain the strength and resilience needed to navigate the challenges of parenting.

Ultimately, when we empower parents, we empower our children. By recognizing our role as their first and most influential teachers, we hold the power to shape their values, beliefs, and future success. Let us embrace this responsibility with purpose and determination, for our children are the architects of tomorrow.

Conclusion,

"Parenting with Purpose: Nurturing Your Child's Potential" has been a guidebook to empower parents on their journey of raising children. By equipping ourselves with knowledge, fostering self-reflection, building strong bonds, and seeking support, we can create an environment that nurtures our child's potential. Remember, as parents, we play a pivotal role in shaping the future of our children, and through empowerment, we can unlock their limitless possibilities.